My Innovative Keto Chaffles Cookbook

A Full Collection of Keto Chaffle Dishes

Imogene Cook

TABLE OF CONTENTS

30 DAYS MEAL PLAN

DAYS	BREAKFAST	LUNCH	DINNER	DESSERT
1	Breakfast chaffle sandwich	Chicken Bites with Chaffles	Maple Chaffle	Apple Cinnamon Chaffles
2	Peanut butter and jelly chaffles	Crunchy Fish and Chaffle Bites	Cinnamon Chaffle	Churro Chaffle
3	Halloumi cheese chaffles	Grill Pork Chaffle Sandwich	Creamy Chaffles	Blueberry Chaffles
4	Chaffles benedict	Chaffle & Chicken Lunch Plate	Choco And Spinach Chaffles	Super Easy Chocolate Chaffles
5	Carnivore chaffle	Chaffle Egg Sandwich	Pumpkin Chaffles With Choco Chips	Oreo Cookies Chaffles
6	Cauliflower chaffle	Chaffle Minutes Sandwich	Red Velvet Chaffle	Yogurt Chaffle
7	Hot dog chaffles	Chaffle Cheese Sandwich	Walnuts Lowcarb Chaffles	Brownie Chaffle
8	Omelette	Chicken Zinger Chaffle	Chaffle Cream Cake	Choco Waffle with Cream Cheese
9	Pandan asian chaffles	Double Chicken Chaffles	Simple Peanut Butter Chaffle	Mini Keto Pizza
10	Ham and jalapenos chaffle	Chaffles With Topping	Beginner Brownies Chaffle	Keto Chaffle With Almond Flour

11	Hot ham chaffles	Chaffle With Cheese & Bacon	Holidays Chaffles	Chaffles With Caramelized Apples and Yogurt
12	Bacon & egg chaffles	Grill Beefsteak and Chaffle	Cherry Chocolate Chaffle	Peanut Butter Chaffle Cake
13	Cheese-free breakfast chaffle	Cauliflower Chaffles And Tomatoes	Bacon, Egg & Avocado Chaffle Sandwich	Keto Chaffle With Ice-cream
14	Bacon chaffle omelettes	Chicken Bites with Chaffles	Sausage & Egg Chaffle Sandwich	Chocolate Brownie Chaffles
15	Acocado chaffle toast	Crunchy Fish and Chaffle Bites	Banana Nut Muffin	Chaffle Tortilla
16	Breakfast spinach ricotta chaffles	Grill Pork Chaffle Sandwich	Cinnamon Roll Chaffles	Chicken Chaffle Sandwich
17	Keto chaffle waffle	Chaffle & Chicken Lunch Plate	Choco Chip Lemon Chaffle	Chaffle With Cream Topping
18	Keto chaffle topped with salted caramel syrup	Chaffle Egg Sandwich	Crunchy Coconut Chaffles Cake	Chocolate Chip Chaffle
19	Keto chaffle bacon sandwich	Chaffle Minutes Sandwich	Coffee Flavored Chaffle	Cheese Garlic Chaffle
20	Crispy zucchini chaffle	Chaffle Cheese Sandwich	Italian Sausage Chaffles	Cinnamon Cream Cheese Chaffle
		Chicken	Chaffles With	

21	Peanut butter chaffle	Zinger Chaffle	Strawberry Frosty	Lemon and Vanilla Chaffle
22	Buffalo hummus beef chaffless	Double Chicken Chaffles	Pecan Pumpkin Chaffle	Christmas Smoothie with Chaffles
23	Cauliflower turkey chaffle	Chaffles With Topping	Swiss Bacon Chaffle	Raspberry and Chocolate Chaffle
24	Chaffle with sausage gravy	Chaffle With Cheese & Bacon	Bacon, Olives & Cheddar Chaffle	Keto Belgian Sugar Chaffles
25	Lobster chaffle	Grill Beefsteak and Chaffle	Garlic Chaffle	Pumpkin Chaffle With Maple Syrup
26	Savory pork rind chaffle	Cauliflower Chaffles And Tomatoes	Herby Chaffle Snacks	Maple Syrup & Vanilla Chaffle
27	Bbq chicken chaffle	Chicken Bites with Chaffles	Zucchini Chaffle	Sweet Vanilla Chocolate Chaffle
28	Smoked salmon	Crunchy Fish and Chaffle Bites	Breakfast Spinach Ricotta Chaffles	Thanksgiving Keto Chaffles
29	Grilled steak	Grill Pork Chaffle Sandwich	Pumpkin Chaffle With Frosting	Garlic Cauliflower Chaffle
30	Crab chaffles	Chaffle & Chicken Lunch Plate	Chaffle Strawbery Sandwich	Quick & Easy Blueberry Chaffle

Chicken Bacon Ranch Chaffle

Preparation time: 3 minutes

Cooking time: 8 minutes

Servings: 2

Ingredients:

- 1 egg
- 1/3 cup cooked chicken diced
- 1 piece bacon cooked and crumbled
- 1/3 cup shredded cheddar jack cheese
- 1 teaspoon powdered ranch dressing

Directions:

1. Heat up your Dash mini waffle maker.
2. In a small bowl, mix the egg, ranch dressing, and Monterey Jack Cheese.
3. Add the bacon and chicken and mix well.
4. Add half of the batter into your mini waffle maker and cook for 3-4 minutes. Then cook the rest of the batter to make a second chaffle.

5. Remove from the pan and let sit for 2 minutes.
6. Dip in ranch dressing, sour cream, or enjoy alone.

Nutrition:

Calories 220 Carbohydrates 2.9 g Protein 21.5 g Fat 24.3g

Buffalo Chicken Chaffle Recipe

Preparation time: 10 minutes

Cooking time: 5 minutes

Servings: 6

Ingredients:

- 1 Can Valley Fresh Organic Canned Chicken Breast (5 ounces)
- 2 T Red Hot Wing Sauce
- 2 oz Cream Cheese softened
- 4 T Cheddar Cheese shredded
- 2 T Almond Flour
- 1 T Nutritional Yeast
- 1/2 tsp Baking Powder
- 1 Egg Yolk Can Use whole egg if no allergy
- 1 Flax Egg
- 1 T ground flaxseed,
- 3 T water
- 1/4-1/2 Cup Extra Cheese for the waffle iron

Directions:

1. Make flax egg and set aside to rest.
2. Drain liquid from the canned chicken. Mix all the ingredients together. Sprinkle a little cheese on the waffle iron. Let it sit for a few seconds before adding 3 T of chicken mixture — Cook for 5 minutes.
3. Don't open the waffle iron before the time is up, or you will have a mess. Remove and let cool before adding a drizzle of hot sauce and ranch dressing.

Nutrition:

Calories 320 Carbohydrates 2.9 g Protein 21.5 g Fat 24.3g

Jamaica Chicken Chaffle

Preparation time: 5 minutes

Cooking time: 10 minutes

Servings: 4

Ingredients:

Jamaica Chicken Filling:

- 1 pound organic ground chicken browned or roasted leftover chicken finely chopped
- 2 tablespoons Kerrygold butter
- 1/2 medium onion chopped
- 1 teaspoon granulated garlic
- 1 teaspoon dried thyme
- 1/8 teaspoon black pepper
- 2 teaspoon dried parsley
- 1 teaspoon salt
- 2 teaspoon Walker's Wood Jerk Seasoning
- Hot and Spicy jar type paste
- 1/2 cup chicken broth

Chaffle Ingredients:

- 1/2 cup mozzarella cheese
- 1 tablespoon butter melted
- 1 egg well beaten
- 2 tablespoon almond flour
- 1/4 teaspoon baking powder
- 1/4 teaspoon turmeric
- A pinch of xanthan gum
- A pinch of salt
- A pinch of garlic powder
- A pinch of onion powder

Directions:

1. In a medium saucepan, cook onion in the butter.
2. Add all spices and herbs. Sauté until fragrant.
3. Add chicken.
4. Stir in chicken broth.
5. Cook on low for 10 minutes.
6. Raise temperature to medium-high and reduce liquid until none is left in the bottom of the pan.
7. Enjoy!

Nutrition:

Calories 320 Carbohydrates 2.9 g Protein 21.5 g Fat 24.3g

Wasabi Chaffles

Preparation time: 15 minutes

Cooking time: 15 minutes

Servings: 1

Chaffle Ingredients:

- Classic Chaffle Recipe

Japanese Toppings Ingredients:

- 1 whole avocado, ripe
- 5 slices of pickled ginger
- 1 tbsp of gluten-free soy sauce
- 1/3 of a cup of edamame
- 1/4 of a cup of Japanese pickled vegetables
- 1/2 pound of sushi-grade salmon, sliced
- 1/4 of a tsp of wasabi

Tools: waffle maker, mini or regular sized, one mixing bowl, measuring cups and tablespoons, spatula, non-stick cooking spray (or butter), blender, electric beaters, or whisk.

Directions:

1. Cut the salmon and avocado into thin slices. Set aside.
2. If the edamame is frozen, boil it in a pot of water until done. Set aside.
3. Follow the Classic Chaffle recipe.
4. Once the chaffles are done, pour a tablespoon of soy sauce onto the chaffle and then layer the salmon, avocado, edamame, pickled ginger, pickled vegetables, and wasabi.
5. Enjoy!

Nutrition:

Calories 320 Carbohydrates 2.9 g Protein 21.5 g Fat 24.3g

Loaded Chaffle Nachos

Preparation time: 15 minutes

Cooking time: 15 minutes

Servings: 1

Chaffle Ingredients:

- Classic Chaffle Recipe

Nacho Ingredients:

Taco Meat recipe

- 1 whole avocado, ripe
- 1/2 cup of sour cream
- 1/2 of a cup of cheddar cheese, shredded
- 1/2 an onion
- 1 handful of cilantro, chopped
- 1 lime, cut into wedges
- hot sauce of your choice

Tools: waffle maker, mini or regular sized, one mixing bowl, measuring cups and tablespoons, spatula, non-stick cooking spray (or butter), blender, electric beaters, or whisk.

Directions:

1. Dice the cilantro, lettuce, onions, and limes.
2. Shred the cheese in a bowl. Melt if desired.
3. Follow instructions for the Taco Meat recipe.
4. Follow the Classic Chaffle recipe.
5. Once the chaffles are done, rip them into triangles.
6. Spread the chaffle triangles onto a plate and layer on the sour cream, meat, avocado, onions, cilantro, cheese, and lime.
7. Enjoy!

Nutrition:

Calories 320 Carbohydrates 2.9 g Protein 21.5 g Fat 24.3g

Mozzarella Panini

Preparation time: 15 minutes

Cooking time: 15 minutes

Servings: 1

Chaffle Ingredients:

- Classic Chaffle Recipe

Sandwich Filling Ingredients:

- 1 ounce of mozzarella, thinly sliced
- 1 heirloom tomato, thinly sliced
- 1/4 of a cup of pesto
- 2 fresh basil leaves

Tools: waffle maker, mini or regular sized, one mixing bowl, measuring cups and tablespoons, spatula, non-stick cooking spray (or butter), blender, electric beaters, or whisk.

Directions:

1. Follow the Classic Chaffle recipe.
2. Once the chaffles are done, lay two side by side.

3. Spread the pesto on one, then layer the mozzarella cheese and tomatoes and sandwich together.

Nutrition:

Calories 320 Carbohydrates 2.9 g Protein 21.5 g Fat 24.3g

Lox Bagel Chaffle

Preparation time: 15 minutes

Cooking time: 15 minutes

Servings: 1

Chaffle Ingredients:

Classic Chaffle Recipe or Sweet Chaffle Recipe

- 2 tbsps of Everything Bagel Seasoning

Filling Ingredients:

- 1 ounce of cream cheese
- 1 beefsteak tomato, thinly sliced
- 4-6 ounces of salmon gravlax
- 1 small shallot, thinly sliced
- capers
- 1 tbsp of fresh dill

Tools: waffle maker, mini or regular sized, one mixing bowl, measuring cups and tablespoons, spatula, non-stick cooking spray (or butter), blender, electric beaters, or whisk.

Directions:

1. Slice the tomato and the shallots.
2. Follow the Classic Chaffle recipe and add the everything bagel seasoning.
3. Once the chaffles are done, sprinkle more everything bagel seasoning onto the tops of both chaffles.
4. Lay two chaffles side by side and layer on the cream cheese, salmon, and shallots.
5. Sprinkle dill and capers and sandwich the two chaffles together.
6. Enjoy!

Nutrition:

Calories 320 Carbohydrates 2.9 g Protein 21.5 g Fat 24.3g

Cuban Sandwich Chaffle

Preparation time: 15 minutes

Cooking time: 15 minutes

Servings: 1

Chaffle Ingredients:

- Classic Chaffle Recipe

Cubano Ingredients:

- 1/4 of a pound of ham, cooked and sliced
- 1/4 of a pound of pork, roasted and sliced
- 1/4-pound Swiss cheese, thinly sliced
- 3 dill pickles, sliced in half

Tools: waffle maker, mini or regular sized, three mixing bowls, measuring cups and tablespoons, spatula, non-stick cooking spray (or butter), baking sheet, blender, electric beaters, or whisk.

Directions:

1. Follow the Classic Chaffle recipe.

2. Take two chaffles and lay side by side.

3. Lay on the meat, cheese, and pickles.

4. Sandwich the two chaffles together.

5. Put the sandwich in a toaster oven if you want it hot.

6. Heat for 5 minutes or until cheese is melted.

Parmesan garlic chaffles

Preparation time: 10 minutes

Cooking time: 5 minutes

Servings: 2

Ingredients

- 1/2 cup shredded mozzarella cheese
- 1 whole egg, beaten
- 1/4 cup grated Parmesan cheese
- 1 teaspoon Italian Seasoning
- 1/4 teaspoon garlic powder

Directions

1. Start pre-heating your waffle maker, and let's start preparing the batter.
2. Add in all the ingredients, except for the mozzarella cheese to a bowl and whisk. Add in the cheese and mix until well combined.
3. Spray your waffle plates with nonstick spray and add half the batter to the center.

4. Close the lid and cook for 3-5 minutes, depending on how crispy you want your Chaffles.

5. Serve with a drizzle of olive oil, grated Parmesan cheese and fresh chopped parsley or basil.

Nutrition:

Calories 320 Carbohydrates 2.9 g Protein 21.5 g Fat 24.3g

Key lime Chaffle

Preparation time: 10 minutes

Cooking time: 5 minutes

Servings: 2

Ingredients (for 3 to 4 mini chaffles)

Chaffle ingredients

- 1 egg
- 2 tsp cream cheese room temp
- 1 tsp powdered sweetener swerve or monk fruit
- 1/2 tsp baking powder
- 1/2 tsp lime zest
- 1/4 cup Almond flour
- 1/2 tsp lime extract or 1 tsp fresh squeezed lime juice
- Pinch of salt

Cream Cheese Lime Frosting ingredients

- 4 oz cream cheese softened
- 4 tbs butter
- 2 tsp powdered sweetener swerve or monk fruit
- 1 tsp lime extract

- 1/2 tsp lime zest

Directions:

1. Preheat the mini waffle iron.
2. In a blender add all the chaffle ingredients and blend on high until the mixture is smooth and creamy.
3. Cook each chaffle about 3 to 4 minutes until it's golden brown.
4. While the chaffles are cooking, prepare the frosting.
5. In a small bowl, combine all the ingredients for the frosting and mix until smooth.
6. Allow the chaffles to completely cool before frosting them.

Jicama Loaded Baked Potato Chaffle

Preparation time: 10 minutes

Cooking time: 15 minutes

Servings: 2

Ingredients

- 1 cup cheese of choice
- 2 eggs, whisked
- 1 large jicama root
- 1/2 medium onion, minced
- Salt and Pepper
- 2 garlic cloves, pressed

Directions:

1. Peel jicama and shred in food processor
2. In a large colander, place the shredded jicama, and sprinkle with 1-2 tsp of salt. Mix well and allow to drain.
3. Squeeze out as much liquid as possible

4. Microwave for 5-8 minutes
5. Mix all ingredients together
6. Sprinkle a little cheese on waffle iron, then add 1/3 of the mixture, and sprinkle a little more cheese on top of the mixture.
7. Cook for 5 minutes. Flip and cook 2 more.
8. Top with a dollop of sour cream, bacon pieces, cheese, and chives.

Nutrition:

Calories 320 Carbohydrates 2.9 g Protein 21.5 g Fat 24.3g

Chaffle Mcgriddles

Preparation time: 10 minutes

Cooking time: 5 minutes

Servings: 2

Ingredients

- 1 Egg
- 3/4 cup Shredded Mozzarella
- 1 Sausage Patty
- 1 Slice American Cheese
- 1 tbsp Sugar-Free Flavored Maple Syrup
- 1 tbsp Swerve or Monk fruit (or any sugar replacement of choice)

Directions:

1. Pre-heat your Mini Waffle Maker
2. Beat the egg into a small mixing bowl,
3. Add shredded Mozzarella, Swerve/Monk fruit, Maple Syrup and mix until well combined.

4. Place ~2 tbsp of the resulting egg mix onto the Dash Mini Waffle Maker, close lid and cook for 3 – 4 minutes. Repeat for as many waffles you are making.

5. Meanwhile, follow cooking instructions for sausage patty and place cheese onto patty while still warm to melt.

6. Assemble Chaffle Griddle and enjoy!

Nutrition:

Calories 320 Carbohydrates 2.9 g Protein 21.5 g Fat 24.3g

Light & Crispy Chaffles

Preparation time: 10 minutes

Cooking time: 5 minutes

Servings: 2

Ingredients

- 1 egg
- 1/3 cup cheddar
- 1/4 teaspoon baking powder
- 1/2 teaspoon ground flaxseed
- Shredded parmesan cheese on top and bottom.

Directions:

1. Mix the ingredients together and cook in a mini waffle iron for 4-5 minutes until crispy.
2. Once cool, enjoy your light and crisp Keto waffle.
3. You can experiment with seasonings to the initial mixture depending on the mood of your taste buds.

Chaffle Sandwich With Bacon and Egg

Preparation time: 10 minutes

Cooking time: 5 minutes

Servings: 2

Ingredients

- 1 large egg
- 1/2 cup of shredded cheese
- thick-cut bacon
- fried egg
- sliced cheese

Instructions

1. Preheat your waffle maker.
2. In a small mixing bowl, mix together egg and shredded cheese. Stir until well combined.
3. Pour one half of the waffle batter into the waffle maker. Cook for 3-4 minutes or until golden brown.

Repeat with the second half of the batter.

4.   In a large pan over medium heat, cook the bacon until crispy.

5.   In the same skillet, in 1 tbsp of reserved bacon drippings, fry the egg over medium heat. Cook until desired doneness.

6.   Assemble the sandwich, and enjoy!

Nutrition:

Calories 320 Carbohydrates 2.9 g Protein 21.5 g Fat 24.3g

Rich Creamy Chaffles

Preparation time: 5 minutes

Cooking time: 5 minutes

Servings: 4

Ingredients:

- 1 egg
- ½ cup mozzarella cheese, shredded
- Oil of grease
- Heavy crème
- Salt & pepper to taste

Directions:

1. Heat the waffle maker.
2. Take a bowl add egg or mozzarella cheese and whisk all together. Add some salt or pepper as per taste and mix all together.
3. Spray the oil to grease the waffle maker.
4. Now pour the mixture into the maker and cook for 4 minutes or until golden brown.

5. Repeat the process for the whole batter.
6. Serve the chaffle with heavy crème layer.

Bacon & Cheddar Cheese Chaffles

Preparation time: 5 minutes

Cooking time: 5 minutes

Servings: 6

Ingredients:

- ½ cup almond flour
- 3 bacon strips
- ¼ cup sour cream
- 1 ½ cup cheddar cheese
- ½ cup smoked Gouda cheese
- ½ tsp onion powder
- ½ tsp. baking powder
- ¼ cup oat
- 1 egg
- 1 tbsp. oil
- 1 ½ tbsp. butter
- ¼ tsp. salt
- ½ tsp. parsley

- ¼ tsp. baking soda

Directions:

1. Heat the waffle maker.
2. Take a bowl add almond flour, baking powder, baking soda, onion powder, garlic salt and mix well.
3. In another bowl whisk eggs, bacon, cream, parsley, butter and cheese until well combined.
4. Now pour the mixture over dry ingredients and mix well.
5. Pour the batter over the preheated waffle maker and cook for 5 to 6 minutes or until golden brown.
6. Serve the hot and crispy chaffles.

Nutrition:

Calories 320 Carbohydrates 2.9 g Protein 21.5 g Fat 24.3g

Jalapeno & Bacon Chaffle

Preparation time: 5 minutes

Cooking time: 5 minutes

Servings: 6

Ingredients:

- 3 tbsp. coconut flour
- 1 tsp baking powder
- 3 eggs
- 8 oz. cream cheese
- ¼ tsp salt
- 4 bacon slices
- 2 to 3 jalapeno
- 1 cup cheddar cheese

Directions:

1. Wash the jalapeno and slice them.
2. Take a pan and cook jalapeno until golden brown or crispy.

3.   Take a bowl add flour, baking powder and salt and mix.

4.   In a mixing bowl add cream and beat well until fluffy.

5.   Now in another bowl add egg and whisk them well.

6.   Pour cream, cheese and beat until well combined.

7.   Add the mixture with dry ingredients and make a smooth batter.

8.   After that fold the jalapeno in prepare mixture.

9.   Heat the waffle maker and pour the batter into it.

10.   Cook it for 5 minutes or until golden brown.

11.   Top it with cheese, jalapeno and crème and serve the hot chaffles.

Nutrition:

Calories 320 Carbohydrates 2.9 g Protein 21.5 g Fat 24.3g

Light & Crispy Bagel Chaffle Chips

Preparation time: 5 minutes

Cooking time: 5 minutes

Servings: 4

Ingredients:

- 3 tbsp. parmesan cheese
- 1 tsp oil for grease
- 1 tsp bagel seasoning
- Salt and pepper to taste

Directions:

1. Preheat the waffle maker.
2. Add the parmesan cheese in the pan and melt it well.
3. Now pour the melted parmesan cheese over the waffle maker and sprinkle bagel seasoning over the cheese.
4. Cook the mixture for about 2 to 3 minutes without closing the lid.

5.   Let it settle or turn crispy for 2 minutes then remove and serve the crispy chis crunch.

Nutrition:

Calories 320 Carbohydrates 2.9 g Protein 21.5 g Fat 24.3g

Coconut Flour Waffle

Preparation time: 5 minutes

Cooking time: 5 minutes

Another Chaffle you can prepare is the Coconut flour waffle.

Ingredients

- 8 eggs
- 1/2 cup of butter or coconut oil (melted)
- 1 tsp of vanilla extract
- 1/2 tsp salt
- 1/2 cup of coconut flour

Directions

1. Pre heat the mini waffle maker,
2. Whisk the eggs in a bowl,
3. Then you add the melted butter or coconut oil, cinnamon, vanilla and salt, mix properly then you add the Coconut flour.

4.	Ensure the batter is thick,

5.	Add the mixture into the mini waffle maker and allow to cook till it has a light brown appearance.

6.	Serve with butter or maple syrup.

Nutrition:

Calories 320 Carbohydrates 2.9 g Protein 21.5 g Fat 24.3g

Cream Cheese Waffle

Preparation time: 10 minutes

Cooking time: 5 minutes

Servings: 2

Ingredients

- 2 cups of flour
- 1 tsp baking powder
- 1/8 tsp salt
- 2 tsp light brown sugar
- 4 ounces of 1/3 Less Fat Cream Cheese ,
- 2 eggs
- 1/2 cups of milk
- 2 tablespoons canola oil
- 1/2 tablespoon pure vanilla extract
- 4 tablespoons honey

Directions

1.   First step is to preheat the mini waffle maker.

2. Then you mix the flour, baking powder, salt and light brown sugar; mix thoroughly to ensure uniformity.

3. In your bowl, add the cream cheese and egg yolks; mix until smooth.

4. Then you Add milk, oil and vanilla; mix properly.

5. Add flour mixture to cream cheese mixture and stir until moist.

6. The next step is to Place egg whites in a bowl and beat until it forms a stiff peak.

7. Using a spatula, fold the egg whites gently into the waffle-batter; fold just until thoroughly combined.

8. Pour 1/3-cup of the batter onto the preheated mini waffle iron.

9. Allow to cook for about 2 to 3 minutes, or until it has a light brown appearance

10. Next step is to prepare the Whipped Cream. Pour the heavy cream into a large mixing bowl and beat on until it becomes thick.

11. Add honey and continue to beat until soft peaks form. When ready,

12. Serve waffles topped with Honey Whipped Cream and fresh berries (if you prefer).

Nutrition:

Calories 320 Carbohydrates 2.9 g Protein 21.5 g Fat 24.3g

Keto Taco Chaffle

Preparation time: 10 minutes

Cooking time: 4 minutes

Servings: 2

Ingredients

- 1/2 cup cheese (cheddar or mozzarella), shredded
- 1 egg
- 1/4 teaspoon Italian seasoning
- Taco Meat seasoning for ground beef

You have to prepare your Taco meat separately, you'll need the following ingredients for Taco meat seasoning;

- 1/4 cup chili spowder
- 1/4 cup ground cumin
- 2 tablespoons garlic powder
- 2 tablespoons cocoa powder
- 1 tablespoon onion powder
- 1 tablespoon salt
- 1 teaspoon smoked paprika

Directions

1. You have to Cook your ground beef or ground turkey first Separately. Add all the taco meat seasonings.
2. While making the taco meat, start making the keto chaffles.
3. First step is to Pre-heat the mini waffle maker.
4. Whisk the egg in a small bowl,
5. Add the shredded cheese and seasoning.
6. Place half the chaffle mixture into the mini waffle maker and allow it to cook for about 3 to 4minutes.
7. Repeat and cook the second half of the mixture to make the second chaffle.
8. Add the warm taco meat to your taco chaffle. You can Top it with lettuce, tomatoes, cheese, and serve.

Nutrition:

Calories 120 Carbohydrates 1.9 g Protein 21.5 g Fat 24.3g

Simple Brownie Chaffle

Preparation time: 5 minutes

Cooking time: 3 minutes

Servings: 2

If you love brownies, then you should try this brownie Chaffle recipe which is very easy to make and is ready in few minutes.

Ingredients

- 1 Egg Whisked
- 1/3 cup Mozzarella Cheese Shredded
- 1 ½ tbsp Cocoa Powder Dutch Processed
- 1 tbsp Almond Flour
- 1 tbsp Monk fruit Sweetener
- 1/4 tsp Vanilla extract
- 1/4 tsp Baking Powder
- Pinch of Salt
- 2 tsp Heavy Cream

Directions

1. First step as always is to preheat your mini waffle iron.
2. Next, whisk the egg. Add the dry ingredients.
3. Then add the cheese in a bowl.
4. Then you Pour 1/3 of the batter on the waffle iron.
5. Allow to cook for 3 minutes or until steam stops coming out of the waffle iron.
6. Serve with your favorite low carb toppings.

Nutrition:

Calories 320 Carbohydrates 2.9 g Protein 21.5 g Fat 24.3g

White Bread Keto Chaffle

Preparation time: 5 minutes

Cooking time: 4 minutes

Servings: 2

Ingredients

- 2 egg whites
- cream cheese, melted
- 2 tsp water
- 1/4 tsp baking powder
- 1/4 cup almond flour
- 1 Pinch of salt

Directions

1. Pre-heat the mini waffle maker,
2. Whisk the egg whites together with the cream cheese and water in a bowl.
3. Next step is to add the baking powder, almond flour and salt and whisk until you have a smooth batter. Then you pour half of the batter into the mini waffle maker.

4.   Allow to cook for roughly 4 minutes or until you no longer see steam coming from the waffle maker.

5.   Remove and allow to cool.

Nutrition:

Calories 320 Carbohydrates 2.9 g Protein 21.5 g Fat 24.3g

Cranberry and Brie Chaffle

Preparation time: 10 minutes

Cooking time: 20 minutes

Servings: 4 mini chaffles

Ingredients:

- 4 tablespoons frozen cranberries
- 3 tablespoons swerve sweetener
- 1 cup / 115 grams shredded brie cheese
- 2 eggs, at room temperature

Directions:

1. Take a non-stick waffle iron, plug it in, select the medium or medium-high heat setting and let it preheat until ready to use; it could also be indicated with an indicator light changing its color.

2. Meanwhile, prepare the batter and for this, take a heatproof bowl, add cheese in it, and microwave at high heat setting for 15 seconds or until cheese has softened.

3. Then add sweetener, berries, and egg into the cheese and whisk with an electric mixer until smooth.

4. Use a ladle to pour one-fourth of the prepared batter into the heated waffle iron in a spiral direction, starting from the edges, then shut the lid and cook for 4 minutes or more until solid and nicely browned; the cooked waffle will look like a cake.

5. When done, transfer chaffles to a plate with a silicone spatula and repeat with the remaining batter.

6. Let chaffles stand for some time until crispy and serve straight away.

Nutrition:

Calories 320 Carbohydrates 2.9 g Protein 21.5 g Fat 24.3g

Banana Foster Chaffle

Preparation time: 10 minutes

Cooking time: 20 minutes

Servings: 4 large chaffles

Ingredients:

For Chaffle:

- 1/8 teaspoon cinnamon
- ½ teaspoon banana extract, unsweetened
- 4 teaspoons swerve sweetener
- 1 cup / 225 grams cream cheese, softened
- ½ teaspoon vanilla extract, unsweetened
- 8 eggs, at room temperature

For Syrup:

- 20 drops of banana extract, unsweetened
- 8 teaspoons swerve sweetener
- 20 drops of caramel extract, unsweetened
- 12 drops of rum extract, unsweetened
- 8 tablespoons unsalted butter
- 1/8 teaspoon cinnamon

Directions:

1. Take a non-stick waffle iron, plug it in, select the medium or medium-high heat setting and let it preheat until ready to use; it could also be indicated with an indicator light changing its color.

2. Meanwhile, prepare the batter for chaffle and for this, take a large bowl, crack eggs in it, add sweetener, cream cheese, and all the extracts and then mix with an electric mixer until smooth, let the batter stand for 5 minutes.

3. Use a ladle to pour one-fourth of the prepared batter into the heated waffle iron in a spiral direction, starting from the edges, then shut the lid and cook for 5 minutes or more until solid and nicely browned; the cooked waffle will look like a cake.

4. When done, transfer chaffles to a plate with a silicone spatula, repeat with the remaining batter and let chaffles stand for some time until crispy.

5. Meanwhile, prepare the syrup and for this, take a small heatproof bowl, add butter in it, and microwave at high heat setting for 15 seconds until it melts.

6. Then add remaining ingredients for the syrup and mix until combined.

7. Drizzle syrup over chaffles and then serve.

Nutrition:

Calories 320 Carbohydrates 2.9 g Protein 21.5 g Fat 24.3g

Flaxseed Chaffle

Preparation time: 10 minutes

Cooking time: 20 minutes

Servings: 4 medium chaffles

Ingredients:

- 2 cups ground flaxseed
- 2 teaspoons ground cinnamon
- 1 teaspoon of sea salt
- 1 tablespoon baking powder
- 1/3 cup / 80 ml avocado oil
- 5 eggs, at room temperature
- ½ cup / 120 ml water
- Whipped cream as needed for topping

Directions:

1. Take a non-stick waffle iron, plug it in, select the medium or medium-high heat setting and let it preheat until ready to use; it could also be indicated with an indicator light changing its color.

2. Meanwhile, prepare the batter and for this, take a large bowl and then stir in flaxseed, salt and baking powder until combined.

3. Crack the eggs in a jug, pour in oil and water, whisk these ingredients until blended and then stir this mixture into the flour with the spatula until incorporated and fluffy mixture comes together.

4. Let the batter stand for 5 minutes and then stir in cinnamon until mixed.

5. Use a ladle to pour one-fourth of the prepared batter into the heated waffle iron in a spiral direction, starting from the edges, then shut the lid and cook for 5 minutes or more until solid and nicely browned; the cooked waffle will look like a cake.

6. When done, transfer chaffle to a plate with a silicone spatula and repeat with the remaining batter.

7. Top waffles with whipped cream and then serve straight away.

Nutrition:

Calories 320 Carbohydrates 2.9 g Protein 21.5 g Fat 24.3g

Hazelnut Chaffle

Preparation time: 10 minutes

Cooking time: 30 minutes

Servings: 6 mini chaffles

Ingredients:

- 1 cup / 100 grams hazelnut flour
- ½ teaspoon baking powder
- 2 tablespoons hazelnut oil
- 1 cup / 245 grams almond milk, unsweetened
- 3 eggs, at room temperature

Directions:

1. Take a non-stick waffle iron, plug it in, select the medium or medium-high heat setting and let it preheat until ready to use; it could also be indicated with an indicator light changing its color.

2. Meanwhile, prepare the batter and for this, take a large bowl, add flour in it, stir in the baking powder until mixed and then mix in oil, milk, and egg with an electric mixer until smooth.

3. Use a ladle to pour one-sixth of the prepared batter into the heated waffle iron in a spiral direction, starting from the edges, then shut the lid and cook for 5 minutes or more until solid and nicely browned; the cooked waffle will look like a cake.

4. When done, transfer chaffle to a plate with a silicone spatula and repeat with the remaining batter.

5. Let chaffles stand for some time until crispy and serve straight away.

Nutrition:

Calories 320 Carbohydrates 2.9 g Protein 21.5 g Fat 24.3g

Maple Pumpkin Chaffle

Preparation time: 5 minutes

Cooking time: 4 minutes

Servings: 2

Ingredients:

- 2 eggs
- 3/4 tsp baking powder
- 2 tsp 100% pumpkin puree
- 3/4 tsp pumpkin pie spice
- 4 tsp heavy whipping cream
- 2 tsp sugar-free maple syrup
- 1 tsp coconut flour
- 1/2 cup mozzarella cheese, shredded
- 1/2 tsp vanilla
- Pinch of salt

Directions:

1.   Preheat the waffle maker.
2.   Combine all ingredients in a small mixing bowl.

3. If you're using a mini waffle maker, pour around 1/4 of the batter. Allow to cook for 3-4 minutes.
4. Repeat.

Nutrition:

Calories 320 Carbohydrates 2.9 g Protein 21.5 g Fat 24.3g

Nutty Chaffles

Preparation time: 5 minutes

Cooking time: 5 minutes

Servings: 1

Ingredients:

- 1 egg
- 1 tsp coconut flour
- 1 1/2 tbsp unsweetened cocoa
- 2 tbsp sugar-free sweetener
- 1 tbsp heavy cream
- 1/2 tsp baking powder
- 1/2 tsp vanilla

Directions:

1. Preheat the waffle maker.
2. Combine all the ingredients in a small bowl. Mix well.
3. Pour half the batter into the waffle maker. Allow to cook for 3-5 minutes until golden brown and crispy.
4. Carefully remove and add the remaining batter.

Nutrition:

Calories 320 Carbohydrates 2.9 g Protein 21.5 g Fat 24.3g

Crispy Chaffle

Preparation time: 5 minutes

Cooking time: 5 minutes

Servings: 1

Ingredients:

- 2 eggs
- 1/2 cup parmesan cheese
- 1 tsp everything but the bagel seasoning
- 1/2 cup mozzarella cheese
- 2 tsp almond flour

Directions:

1. Preheat the waffle maker.
2. Sprinkle the mozzarella cheese onto the waffle maker. Let it melt and cook for 30 seconds until crispy. Remove this from the waffle maker.
3. Using a whisk, combine eggs, parmesan, almond flour, seasoning, and the toasted cheese in a small bowl.
4. Pour the batter into the waffle maker.

5. Allow the batter to cook for 3-4 minutes until crispy and golden brown in color.

Nutrition:

Calories 320 Carbohydrates 2.9 g Protein 21.5 g Fat 24.3g

Strawberry and Cream Cheese Low-Carb Keto Waffles

Preparation time: 5 minutes

Cooking time: 5 minutes

Servings: 2

Ingredients:

- 2 tsp coconut flour
- 4 tsp monk fruit
- 1/4 tsp baking powder
- 1 egg
- 1 oz cream cheese, softened
- 1/2 tsp vanilla extract
- 1/4 cup strawberries

Directions:

1. Preheat the waffle maker.
2. In a bowl put in the coconut flour, then add the baking powder and the monk fruit.

3. Add in the egg, cream cheese, and vanilla extract. Mix well with a whisk.

4. Pour the batter into the preheated waffle maker and allow to cook for 3-4 minutes.

5. Allow chaffles to cool before topping with strawberries.

Nutrition:

Calories 320 Carbohydrates 2.9 g Protein 21.5 g Fat 24.3g

Pumpkin Chaffle With Cream Cheese Glaze

Preparation time: 5 minutes

Cooking time: 5 minutes

Servings: 1

Ingredients:

- 1 egg
- 1/2 cup mozzarella cheese
- 1/2 tsp pumpkin pie spice
- 1 tbsp pumpkin

For the cream cheese frosting:

- 2 tbsp cream cheese, softened at room temperature
- 2 tbsp monk fruit
- 1/2 tsp vanilla extract

Directions:

1. Preheat the waffle maker.
2. Whip the egg in a small bowl.

3.   Add cheese, pumpkin, and pumpkin pie spice to the whipped egg and mix well.

4.   Add half the batter to the waffle maker and allow to cook for 3-4 minutes.

5.   While waiting for the chaffle to cook, combine all the ingredients for the frosting in another bowl. Continue mixing until a smooth and creamy consistency is reached. Feel free to add more butter if you prefer a buttery taste.

Nutrition:

Calories 320 Carbohydrates 2.9 g Protein 21.5 g Fat 24.3g Allow the chaffle to cool before frosting it with cream cheese.

Crunch Cereal Cake Chaffle

Preparation time: 10 minutes

Cooking time: 5 minutes

Servings: 1

(Does not include the toppings)

Ingredients:

For the chaffles:

- 1 egg
- 2 tbsp almond flour
- 1/2 tsp coconut flour
- 1 tbsp butter, melted
- 1 tbsp cream cheese, softened
- 1/4 tsp vanilla extract
- 1/4 tsp baking powder
- 1 tbsp confectioners' sweetener
- 1/8 tsp xanthan gum

For the toppings:

- 20 drops captain cereal flavoring
- Whipped cream

Directions:

1. Preheat the mini waffle maker.
2. Blend or mix all the chaffles ingredients until the consistency is creamy and smooth. Allow to rest for a few minutes so that the flour absorbs the liquid ingredients.
3. Scoop out 2-3 tbsp of batter and put it into the waffle maker. Allow to cook for 2-3 minutes.
4. Top the cooked chaffles with freshly whipped cream.
5. Add syrup and drops of Captain Cereal flavoring for a great flavor.

Nutrition:

Calories 120 Carbohydrates 1.9 g

Spinach Chaffles

Preparation time: 10 minutes

Cooking Time: 20 Minutes

Servings: 2

Ingredients:

- 1 large organic egg, beaten
- 1 cup ricotta cheese, crumbled
- ½ cup Mozzarella cheese, shredded
- ¼ cup Parmesan cheese, grated
- 4 ounces frozen spinach, thawed and squeezed
- 1 garlic clove, minced
- Salt and freshly ground black pepper, to taste

Directions:

1. Preheat a mini waffle iron and then grease it.
2. In a medium bowl, place all ingredients and mix until well combined.
3. Place ¼ of the mixture into preheated waffle iron and cook for about 4-5 minutes or until golden brown.

4.   Repeat with the remaining mixture.

5.   Serve warm.

Nutrition:

Calories:139   Net   Carb:4.3g   Fat:8.1g   Saturated   Fat:4g
Carbohydrates: 4.7g Dietary Fiber: 0.4g Sugar: 0.4g Protein:
12.5g

Ground Beef Chaffles

Preparation time: 10 minutes

Cooking Time: 20 Minutes

Servings: 2

Ingredients:

- ½ cup cooked grass-fed ground beef
- 3 cooked bacon slices, chopped
- 2 organic eggs
- ½ cup Cheddar cheese, shredded
- ½ cup Mozzarella cheese, shredded
- 2 teaspoons steak seasoning

Directions:

1. Preheat a mini waffle iron and then grease it.
2. In a medium bowl, place all ingredients and mix until well combined.
3. Place ¼ of the mixture into preheated waffle iron and cook for
4. about 4-5 minutes or until golden brown.

5.   Repeat with the remaining mixture.

6.   Serve warm.

Nutrition:

Calories:214 Net Carb:0.g Fat:12g Saturated Fat:

5.7g Carbohydrates: 0.5g Dietary Fiber: g Sugar: 0.2g Protein: 2.1g

Chicken & Bacon Chaffles

Preparation time: 6 minutes

Cooking Time: 8 Minutes

Servings: 2

Ingredients:

- 1 organic egg, beaten
- 1/3 cup grass-fed cooked chicken, chopped
- 1 cooked bacon slice, crumbled
- 1/3 cup Pepper Jack cheese, shredded
- 1 teaspoon powdered ranch dressing

Directions:

1. Preheat a mini waffle iron and then grease it.
2. In a medium bowl, place all ingredients and with a fork, mix until well combined.
3. Place half of the mixture into preheated waffle iron and cook for about 4 minutes or until golden brown.
4. Repeat with the remaining mixture.
5. Serve warm.

Nutrition:

Calories:145   Net   Carb:0.9g   Fat:9.4g   Saturated   Fat:4.
Carbohydrates: 1g Dietary Fiber: 0.1g Sugar: 0.2g Protein: 14.3g

Belgium Chaffles

Preparation time: 5 minutes

Cooking Time: 6 Minutes

Servings: 2

Ingredients:

- 2 eggs
- 1 cup Reduced-fat Cheddar cheese, shredded

Directions:

1. Turn on waffle maker to heat and oil it with cooking spray.
2. Whisk eggs in a bowl, add cheese. Stir until well-combined.
3. Pour mixture into waffle maker and cook for 6 minutes until done.
4. Let it cool a little to crisp before serving.

Nutrition: Carbs: 2 g ; Fat: 33 g ; Protein: 44 g ; Calories: 460

Salmon Chaffles

Preparation time: 6 minutes

Cooking Time: 10 Minutes

Servings: 2

Ingredients:

- 1 large egg
- ½ cup shredded mozzarella
- 1 Tbsp cream cheese
- 2 slices salmon
- 1 Tbsp everything bagel seasoning

Directions:

1. Turn on waffle maker to heat and oil it with cooking spray.
2. Beat egg in a bowl, then add ½ cup mozzarella.
3. Pour half of the mixture into the waffle maker and cook for 4 minutes.
4. Remove and repeat with remaining mixture.
5. Let chaffles cool, then spread cream cheese, sprinkle

6.   with seasoning, and top with salmon.

Nutrition:

Carbs: 3 g ; Fat: 10 g ; Protein: 5 g ; Calories: 201

Chaffle Pork Rinds Sandwich

Preparation time: 10 minutes

Cooking Time: 00 Minutes

Servings: 2

Ingredients:

For the chicken:

- ¼ lb boneless and skinless chicken thigh
- ⅛ tsp salt
- ⅛ tsp black pepper
- ½ cup almond flour
- 1 egg
- 3 oz unflavored pork rinds
- 2 cup vegetable oil for deep frying

For the brine:

- 2 cup of water
- 1 Tbsp salt

For the sauce:

- 2 Tbsp sugar-free ketchup
- 1½ Tbsp Worcestershire Sauce
- 1 Tbsp oyster sauce
- 1 tsp swerve/monk fruit

For the chaffle:

- 2 egg
- 1 cup shredded mozzarella cheese

Directions:

1. Add brine ingredients in a large mixing bowl.
2. Add chicken and brine for 1 hour.
3. Pat chicken dry with a paper towel. Sprinkle with salt and pepper. Set aside.
4. Mix ketchup, oyster sauce, Worcestershire sauce, and swerve in a small mixing bowl.
5. Pulse pork rinds in a food processor, making fine crumbs.
6. Fill one bowl with flour, a second bowl with beaten eggs, and a third with crushed pork rinds.
7. Dip and coat each thigh in: flour, eggs, crushed pork rinds. Transfer on holding a plate.
8. Add oil to cover ½ inch of frying pan. Heat to 375°F.

9.   Once oil is hot, reduce heat to medium and add chicken. Cooking time depends on the chicken thickness.

10.   Transfer to a drying rack.

11.   Turn on waffle maker to heat and oil it with

12.   cooking spray.

13.   Beat egg in a small bowl.

14.   Place ⅛ cup of cheese on waffle maker, then add¼ of the egg mixture and top with ⅛ cup of cheese.

15.   Cook for 3-4 minutes.

16.   Repeat for remaining batter.

17.   Top chaffles with chicken katsu, 1 Tbsp sauce, and another piece of chaffle.

Nutrition:

Carbs: 12 g ; Fat: 1 g ; Protein: 2 g ; Calories: 57

Pork Rind Chaffles

Preparation time: 6 minutes

Cooking Time: 10 Minutes

Servings: 2

Ingredients:

- 1 organic egg, beaten
- ½ cup ground pork rinds
- 1/3 cup Mozzarella cheese, shredded
- Pinch of salt

Directions:

1. Preheat a mini waffle iron and then grease it.
2. In a bowl, place all the ingredients and beat until well combined.
3. Place half of the mixture into preheated waffle iron and cook for about 5 minutes or until golden brown.
4. Repeat with the remaining mixture.
5. Serve warm.

Nutrition:

Calories:91   Net   Carb:0.3g   Fat:5.9g   Saturated   Fat:2.3g
Carbohydrates: 0.3g Dietary Fiber: 0g Sugar: 0.2g Protein: 9.2g

Chaffle Bruschetta

Preparation time: 5 minutes

Cooking Time: 5 Minutes

Servings: 2

Ingredients:

- ½ cup shredded mozzarella cheese
- 1 whole egg beaten
- ¼ cup grated Parmesan cheese
- 1 tsp Italian Seasoning
- ¼ tsp garlic powder

For the toppings:

- 3-4 cherry tomatoes, chopped
- 1 tsp fresh basil, chopped
- Splash of olive oil
- Pinch of salt

Directions:

1. Turn on waffle maker to heat and oil it with cooking spray.
2. Whisk all chaffle ingredients, except mozzarella, in a bowl.
3. Add in cheese and mix.
4. Add batter to waffle maker and cook for 5 minutes.
5. Mix tomatoes, basil, olive oil, and salt. Serve over the top of chaffles.

Nutrition:

Carbs: 2 g ; Fat: 24 g ;Protein: 34 g ;Calories: 352

Cheddar Protein Chaffles

Servings: 8

Cooking Time: 40 Minutes

Ingredients:

- ½ cup golden flax seeds meal
- ½ cup almond flour
- 2 tablespoons unsweetened whey protein powder
- 1 teaspoon organic baking powder
- Salt and freshly ground black pepper, to taste
- ¾ cup Cheddar cheese, shredded
- 1/3 cup unsweetened almond milk
- 2 tablespoons unsalted butter, melted
- 2 large organic eggs, beaten

Directions:

1.   Preheat a mini waffle iron and then grease it.
2.   In a large bowl, place flax seeds meal, flour, protein powder and baking powder and mix well.
3.   Stir in the Cheddar cheese.

4. In another bowl, place the remaining ingredients and beat until well combined.
5. Add the egg mixture into the bowl with flax seeds meal mixture and mix until well combined.
6. Place desired amount of the mixture into preheated waffle iron and cook for about 4-5 minutes or until golden brown.
7. Repeat with the remaining mixture.
8. Serve warm.

Nutrition:

Calories:187   Net   Carb:1.8g   Fat:14.5g   Saturated   Fat:5g
Carbohydrates: 4. Dietary Fiber: 3.1g Sugar: 0.4g Protein: 8g

Chicken & Ham Chaffles

Preparation time: 10 minutes

Cooking Time: 16 Minutes

Servings: 2

Ingredients:

- ¼ cup grass-fed cooked chicken, chopped
- 1 ounce sugar-free ham, chopped
- 1 organic egg, beaten
- ¼ cup Swiss cheese, shredded
- ¼ cup Mozzarella cheese, shredded

Directions:

1. Preheat a mini waffle iron and then grease it.
2. In a medium bowl, place all ingredients and mix until well combined.
3. Place ¼ of the mixture into preheated waffle iron and cook for about 4 minutes or until golden brown.
4. Repeat with the remaining mixture.
5. Serve warm.

Nutrition:

Calories:71 Net Carb:0.7g Fat:4.2g Saturated Fat:2g Carbohydrates: 0.8g Dietary Fiber: 0.1g Sugar: 0.2g Protein: 7.4g

Herb Chaffles

Preparation time: 10 minutes

Cooking Time: 12 Minutes

Servings: 2

Ingredients:

- 4 tablespoons almond flour
- 1 tablespoon coconut flour
- 1 teaspoon mixed dried herbs
- ½ teaspoon organic baking powder
- ¼ teaspoon garlic powder
- ¼ teaspoon onion powder
- Salt and ground black pepper, to taste
- ¼ cup cream cheese, softened
- 3 large organic eggs
- ½ cup cheddar cheese, grated
- 1/3 cup Parmesan cheese, grated

Directions:

1. Preheat a waffle iron and then grease it.
2. In a bowl, mix together the flours, dried herbs, baking powder, and seasoning, and mix well.
3. In a separate bowl, put cream cheese and eggs and beat until well combined.
4. Add the flour mixture, cheddar, and Parmesan cheese, and mix until well combined.
5. Place the desired amount of the mixture into preheated waffle iron and cook for about 2–3 minutes.
6. Repeat with the remaining mixture.
7. Serve warm.

Nutrition:

Calories 240 Net Carb: g Total Fat 19 g Saturated Fat 5 g Cholesterol 176 mg Sodium 280 mg Total Carbs 4 g Fiber 1.6 g Sugar 0.7 g Protein 12.3 g

Scallion Chaffles

Preparation time: 6 minutes

Cooking Time: 8 Minutes

Servings: 2

Ingredients:

- 1 organic egg, beaten
- ½ cup Mozzarella cheese, shredded
- 1 tablespoon scallion, chopped
- ½ teaspoon Italian seasoning

Directions:

1. Preheat a mini waffle iron and then grease it.
2. In a medium bowl, place all ingredients and with a fork, mix until well combined.
3. Place half of the mixture into preheated waffle iron and cook for about 4 minutes or until golden brown.
4. Repeat with the remaining mixture.
5. Serve warm.

Nutrition:

Calories:5et   Carb:0.7g   Fat:3.8g   Saturated   Fat:1.5g
Carbohydrates: 0.8g Dietary Fiber: 0.g Sugar: 0.3g Protein: 4.8g

Eggs Benedict Chaffle

Preparation time: 6 minutes

Cooking Time: 10 Minutes

Servings: 2

Ingredients:

For the chaffle:

- 2 egg whites
- 2 Tbsp almond flour
- 1 Tbsp sour cream
- ½ cup mozzarella cheese

For the hollandaise:

- ½ cup salted butter
- 4 egg yolks
- 2 Tbsp lemon juice

For the poached eggs:

- 2 eggs
- 1 Tbsp white vinegar
- 3 oz deli ham

Directions:

1. Whip egg white until frothy, then mix in remaining ingredients.
2. Turn on waffle maker to heat and oil it with cooking spray.
3. Cook for 7 minutes until golden brown.
4. Remove chaffle and repeat with remaining batter.
5. Fill half the pot with water and bring to a boil.
6. Place heat-safe bowl on top of pot, ensuring bottom doesn't touch the boiling water.
7. Heat butter to boiling in a microwave.
8. Add yolks to double boiler bowl and bring to boil.
9. Add hot butter to the bowl and whisk briskly. Cook until the egg yolk mixture has thickened.
10. Remove bowl from pot and add in lemon juice.
11. Set aside.
12. Add more water to pot if needed to make the poached eggs (water should completely cover the eggs). Bring to a simmer. Add white vinegar to water.
13. Crack eggs into simmering water and cook for 1 minute 30 seconds. Remove using slotted spoon.
14. Warm chaffles in toaster for 2-3 minutes. Top with ham, poached eggs, and hollandaise sauce.

Nutrition:

Carbs: 4 g ; Fat: 26 g ; Protein: 26 g ; Calories: 365

Chicken Bacon Chaffle

Preparation time: 6 minutes

Cooking Time: 5 Minutes

Servings: 2

Ingredients:

- 1 egg
- ⅓ cup cooked chicken, diced
- 1 piece of bacon, cooked and crumbled
- ⅓ cup shredded cheddar jack cheese
- 1 tsp powdered ranch dressing

Directions:

1. Turn on waffle maker to heat and oil it with cooking spray.
2. Mix egg, dressing, and Monterey cheese in a small bowl.
3. Add bacon and chicken.
4. Add half of the batter to the waffle maker and cook for 3-minutes.

5.   Remove and cook remaining batter to make a second chaffle.

6.   Let chaffles sit for 2 minutes before serving.

Nutrition:

Carbs: 2 g ; Fat: 14 g ; Protein: 16 g ; Calories: 200

Bacon & Veggies Chaffles

Servings: 6

Cooking Time: 24 Minutes

Ingredients:

- 2 cooked bacon slices, crumbled
- ½ cup frozen chopped spinach, thawed and squeezed
- ½ cup cauliflower rice
- 2 organic eggs
- ½ cup Cheddar cheese, shredded
- ½ cup Mozzarella cheese, shredded
- ¼ cup Parmesan cheese, grated
- 1 tablespoon butter, melted
- 1 teaspoon garlic powder
- 1 teaspoon onion powder

Directions:

1. Preheat a mini waffle iron and then grease it.
2. In a bowl, place all the ingredients except blueberries and beat until well combined.

3. Fold in the blueberries.

4. Divide the mixture into 6 portions.

5. Place 1 portion of the mixture into preheated waffle iron and cook for about 3-4 minutes or until golden brown.

6. Repeat with the remaining mixture.

7. Serve warm.

Nutrition:

Calories:10et   Carb:1.2g   Fat:8.4g   Saturated   Fat:4.6g
Carbohydrates: 1.5g Dietary Fiber: 0.3g Sugar: 0.6g Protein: 7.1g

Garlic Cheese Chaffle Bread Sticks

Servings: 8

Cooking Time: 5 Minutes

Ingredients:

- 1 medium egg
- ½ cup mozzarella cheese, grated
- 2 Tbsp almond flour
- ½ tsp garlic powder
- ½ tsp oregano
- ½ tsp salt

For the toppings:

- 2 Tbsp butter, unsalted softened
- ½ tsp garlic powder
- ¼ cup grated mozzarella cheese
- 2 tsp dried oregano for sprinkling

Directions:

1. Turn on waffle maker to heat and oil it with cooking spray.
2. Beat egg in a bowl.
3. Add mozzarella, garlic powder, flour, oregano, and salt, and mix.
4. Spoon half of the batter into the waffle maker.
5. Close and cook for minutes. Remove cooked chaffle.
6. Repeat with remaining batter.
7. Place chaffles on a tray and preheat the grill.
8. Mix butter with garlic powder and spread over the chaffles.
9. Sprinkle mozzarella over top and cook under the broiler for 2-3 minutes, until cheese has melted.

Nutrition:

Carbs: 1 g ; Fat: 7 g ; Protein: 4 g ; Calories: 74

Simple Savory Chaffles

Preparation time: 6 minutes

Cooking Time: 8 Minutes

Servings: 4

Ingredients:

- 1 large organic egg, beaten
- ½ cup Cheddar cheese, shredded
- Pinch of salt and freshly ground black pepper

Directions:

1. Preheat a mini waffle iron and then grease it.
2. In a bowl, place all the ingredients and beat until well combined.
3. Place half of the mixture into preheated waffle iron and cook for about 4 minutes or until golden brown.
4. Repeat with the remaining mixture.
5. Serve warm.

Nutrition:

Calories:150 Net Carb:0. Fat:11.9g Saturated Fat:6.7g Carbohydrates: 0.6g Dietary Fiber: 0g Sugar: 0.3g Protein: 10.2g

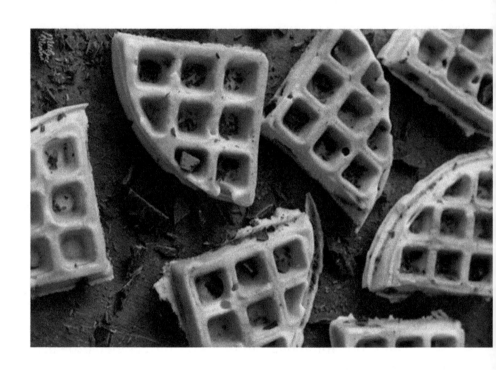

Ingram Content Group UK Ltd.
Milton Keynes UK
UKHW020018190423
420401UK00005B/129